Stay Lit

Quotes to Enliven One's Sense of Presence: Book One

By Darnell P. Smith

Copyright © 2022 Darnell P. Smith

All rights reserved.

ISBN: 979-8-9906786-3-7

DEDICATION

This book is dedicated to the memory of my older brother, Percell Jr. and to all of those souls whose transition came all too soon.

CONTENTS

Acknowledgments

Prelude

1. Life Lessons & Concepts 1

2. Words of Encouragement 159

3. Food for Thought 225

4. Connection to Nature 307

Author Index

ACKNOWLEDGMENTS

First and foremost, I give thanks to the Spirit of our Creator that is present and clearly visible inside of people. These vessels are the bright lights who have endured and overcome the traumas of this world. Through the storms of life that we all must travel, they have been the signpost directing me toward my blessings. With each encounter, trial and tribulation, their light has been the extended and helpful hand. A hand that is their presence. A simple smile or other form of acknowledgement, recognition, or gesture. A real gift of sorts giving me the needed fuel to fulfill my purpose.

Secondly, I'd like to thank Ms. Chelsey J. Macklin for removing the load off of my back and doing what I could not. I might have authored these words, but she was the person who brought this book to its completion. She edited, outlined, compiled, and formulated my writings. When I was lost, she carried my work to its completion. Ms. Chelsey, who I never personally met or had spoken to directly, was God-sent and is my blessing. When my writings were introduced to Chelsey, she immediately understood and felt the necessity of my work and puzzled together the pieces of what is the first of three books from writings already composed. I was introduced to her by a mutual friend, Steven "Flow" Pacheco, who I've been blessed to see mature from a teenager to what he calls "a grown ass man" and he strives to make everyone around him better. He represents true servant leadership, and he makes the impossible happen. His gift to me was being a connector. Anyone reading and benefitting from my work have these two people directly to thank.

Thirdly, I would like to thank those people I call family. I give thanks to the hundreds of young people that have allowed me to have access to both their hearts and minds. It's one thing to have an intention at being of service to another, but it's always clearly up to them to remove their armor. It's very difficult to pour into another if they have a lid covering their container. The energy I give is always given back in equal or greater measure. A few honorable mentions are David Lee, Shareef, the rest of the Pretty SB Skate Crew, Justin, Elias, Ka'shan, Jahlil, Joseph, Bakary, Bonnito, Yuya, Dante, and Cogent.

Finally, I'd like to give thanks to the foundation of my life. The better part of me, my wife Sherniece, who over the last four years has saved the world from my every misspelling and improper use of grammar and other debaucheries of the

English language that I cannot mention. All of us are called to be of service to another. My every effort in my work is to lend my light to the creation of a better world for my daughters Epy and Ray, as well as my niece K.K.. I give thanks to my parents, Percell and Carrie, who have always supported me, although they struggled to understand me.

PRELUDE

I am the product of many storms. A product of scenarios, as a child, I found to be confusing. A product of circumstances that did not make sense and did not correlate with what I was feeling. Along this road, we all travel. My own sense of right and wrong conflicted with much of what I was told. This world sought to carry me in one direction but something within me never agreed. I always sought another answer.

Still, I did my best to comply with what I was told, and I was obedient to my parent's directives and their social influences but there was always something tossed into the mix of what I consumed that caused me to question everything. Most of my life, these feelings stirred inside me. A sense of what was just and what was not conflicted with my reality. I knew of God- not in a religious way or the way that I know God now. Back then, I did not know the importance of ancestors. I saw very little existence of anything that mirrored the energy that existed in me. Every expression had its own box, into which anyone could be placed. Imagine the feeling of not having a space where you felt at home. Not even within the confines of my own body did I ever feel like I belonged.

    Even more confusing was the energy that came from others. These billboard expressions that people wear on their faces felt like lies. Those expressions you get when first introduced to someone. The fake hug, fake smile, the fake kiss on the cheek. Those social responses that meet you as you walk down any street. There was always a tension I felt yet could never clearly see. Those vibes, absent of happiness, have always been the energies that haunted me. They felt like the ocean's waters- cold and deep. I could feel those in the crowd who seemed like they were gasping their last breath. All of us seemed beaten down, as if encountering the waves swallowing water with our every breath. The feeling of drowning. A feeling of being overwhelmed was a normal part of my reality. I knew very little then, compared to what I know now. This sensation that I felt was what others called anxiety.

    The expressions of the defeated worn like hammered African metal masks. People seemed as though they didn't want you to get but so close to them. A true sense of being connected became an estranged feeling. We were all being coveted by a cultural web- a quilt not of our own making and absent of any anointing or symbols for our protection. These coverings received were no different than those given to our indigenous ancestors. The ones received laced with smallpox and other diseases in them. What type of being could do such a thing? The type whose governance is controlled by greed and trickery. A spiritless people consumed with hate. If there is a fear of a virus to be contracted, it would be the one that has me to be something other than human. The fear of becoming one of the walking dead. This is the danger consuming our planet that is all too real.

In my teens, I was among peers who thought of me as respectful, safe, and nice. They thought I shouldn't have any problems and should consider myself okay. But little could those who thought their circumstances worse than mine understand, that there is an equivalent hell to wherever you stand. The fact that I had two hard working parents and they had one or none. All came with its own challenges. Each of us wanting to be the other. With all of us thinking the other had it better. I could remember wanting to be the kid in the projects, allowed to run what I thought was "wild" and without rule, while they, on the other hand, probably wanted what I had: a home of their own with two working parents, discipline, and rules. I could remember my peers that came from households like mine being the ones trying the hardest to be tough in the street. Many of them were killed or went to jail. With their deaths died the hopes and dreams of their families. Yet, from the other side, I saw young people attempting to climb out of their circumstance and condition. The fact of not having anything for themselves had them work harder to get what I already had but did not appreciate. It's interesting how we look at a picture and see it through different lenses. These perceived social standings had us seeing the same thing from different positions.

    The conflicts I encountered in my life sculpted my character. Much of what shaped me came from a feeling that spewed from the hate around me. This world's institutions, systems, fabricated culture, and rituals inclusive of its citizenry and rebels, who are no more than minions, and by-products who exist to maintain the status quo. This is the hate I know. This erupting fire and ice that burns and numbs is the energy that shaped my reality. People wear masks because it is their armor. They've worn them so long that it has become the skin that they are in, altering their true character. We all keep hidden and struggle to maintain that part of ourselves that is only human.

My journey through life has been an attempt at attaining and maintaining a sense of connection to something greater. A sense of being, belonging, knowing, and understanding my relationship with my Creator. This has always been my pursuit. Asking these questions: *Why am I here? Why am I alive?* As early as the age of five, I could remember asking my father, "*Why were we born to die?*"

Throughout my life's journey, these would be the questions that I sought answers to. So, enclosed in this book are my opinions, thoughts, and ideologies that I have learned that I would now like to share with you. Enjoy the journey.

FOREWORD

Imagine the sounds of loud thunder booms in the distance. There are storm clouds filled with cleansing rain forming that must be seen, felt, and heard. Have you ever had thunder rise up inside of your chest? The heavy, mysterious sounds accompanied by bolts of lightning strikes through gray clouds, setting things aflame that were lit by the illuminating light and fire.

I met Darnell through our words and spirits that were full of bright energy before I got to meet him in the physical space. This fact alone should let you in on the depth, power, and liberation you are about to receive, as his being and writing are effortless conduits. On a random but not-so-random afternoon in March 2022, I received a call that I was pleasantly surprised by and, at the same time, not yet in recognition of what strong triangle offense was created and the pure, intricate enchantment that was about to take place. I was offered to help curate the manual and companion that you are currently holding within your hands. What was once a concept, a hoarding of thoughts and concepts, a vision, and a dream, is now being seen as real and tangible for all to see. How about that? Shortly after we met virtually, even though Darnell and I had not ever once met in this physical realm until after months of carefully piecing together Stay Lit: Book One, on the back of the sample book cover that Darnell sent me was his author photo. He looked familiar. I had no prior knowledge of his earthly existence until this fated meeting. A meeting of long-lost family. Soul recognition.

Darnell is a rooted channel for wisdom in this dense realm, using very few words that may go over our head's if we're not paying attention. His vessel is locked into source knowledge with buckets full of humility and he makes us think until we're unable to think anymore. It's all there for us to see. A natural specimen and honorary candidate for gathering the gifts of the Earth- the heart, the mind, the soul, as well as natural processes. Touching delicate and forgotten parts of us with fingertips that we cannot see. Whispers to the core of who we are, beyond flesh.

With lasting feelings of home, these writings will assist us in translating what our internal doorstep looks like, although escalator-like: forever evolving and seemingly going nowhere fast but steady if we just keep moving through with newfound clarity. Peeking at the intricate details of what is housed inside of our chests' through remembrance- the gems we can't see but we are able to recognize if we choose. Mosaic glasses that make our personal temple glow and lit on fire for us to see rainbows of truth ablaze.

    As you read, through the distant rumblings of thunder and flashes of lightning, may the fire in you be ignited through the fortitude of seeing clearly through Brother Smith's pen, paper, and all-seeing eye. May we take these words and run with our batons in a race that we are destined to win. Staying lit through blackouts, divine forgetfulness, and obstacles on the path. To be alive is to see, to hear, and to feel. Your fire is not meant to be hidden or tamed. Allow these pages to penetrate the deepest parts of you and may we feel alive, once again.

                      Sending love, peace, and power,
                             Chelsey J. Macklin

1 LIFE LESSONS AND CONCEPTS

STAY LIT BY DARNELL P. SMITH: BOOK ONE

"The pathway to ease is through difficulty."

"Every word we speak is a prayer and everything we consume is a sacrament."

"Truth be told, everybody needs a friend that influences them to break the rules and in doing so, provides them with a "safe space" to grow."

"Parents, with their concerns, unknowingly can do more harm than good when they overprotect their children. It's almost like tying a noose around their neck that slowly tightens with each descent. Children have an innate knowledge that moves them to explore. Beating, threatening, incarcerating, manipulating, and demeaning does little to diminish this God-given desire. We are here to learn and grow. If our intention is to protect our children, we must orchestrate their learning. When letting go, we must set the stage, introducing them to a community that includes both hero and villain so that our children's intuitive understanding develops in a way that they learn through their own reasoning."

"How many times do you wake up in the night to the horrors of a decision you wish you'd never spoken? Rest your weary eyes and lose not a second more of any sleep. Though the dramas of life are uncertain, rest assured that flowers still grow from the shit we create… even when it stinks. Think less! Ask the Creator for forgiveness from those you have sinned against and move on."

"Death is an unavoidable tragedy, and it is met best with a life of loving, giving, encouraging, guiding, smiling, remaining poised through turbulence, making light of difficulty, extending goodwill, and laughter along the life's path. Death is not the end but the new beginning."

"Let us stop this game of hurting one another. Using our dicks as sticks and vaginas as bait. We were meant to be connected with one another, but not in a way where our life producing assets are weaponized."

"Why are you hard as stone? No life animates from the clay that you are. Your physical demeanor is a scream for help but when help arrives, you lock it out. You gaze proudly at what you've become- a living breathing statue. You hide within your sculpted sense of perfection. I see you. I see the lies hidden underneath. I know the gift that you are, but not even I can unlock the combination you have created. Your shit is password protected in every way. So, here's what I'm going to do: I'm going to create what they call a milieu. Don't be surprised when I shove you into a pool of water. It won't be me trying to kill you but just the opposite. It will be me setting up the circumstances to watch you break free from your casting. Now, in your panic, as you grab what may be your last breath, the grace of God fills you and the weight you carry begins to lighten. The sense of fear and anger has left you. You rest your body on top of the water, floating and with bright eyes and a clear sky, you choose your direction and begin to swim. Now, how great is that?"

"We go to amusement parks to ride rides that are dangerously safe. We like the sensation of something startling us and taking our breath away. Yet, we'd all wish that life was the same way. Offering us some assurances that, if we take a leap of faith and ride life's rollercoaster, that we'd be safe. Unfortunately, life outside the park doesn't work that way. There are always unknown factors at work that don't permit us the ability to control the outcome. In these situations, we either hope, pray or stand dismayed when confronted with the real rides of life that for most of us are not amusing. Yet, ride we must. Each of us must grab life by its horns and scream. In the exhalation of breath, there is discovery. What do you see? There is a part of you fighting to inhale. Fighting to live. Get out your head and embrace this part of you. When everything else seems to fail, just breathe!"

"We've all had embarrassing moments. Those moments that seem to last an eternity but, in reality, may have been seconds or minutes long. I remember being a kid around 11 or 12 years old, out riding bicycles in Long Island with my younger cousin when I fell in front of a group of people, and they all broke out in laughter. No one seemed to care if I was ok. Blood dripping from my hand and knee didn't seem to capture anyone's attention. My cousin was the only one who checked to see if I was alright, and he's been doing that his whole life. As I brushed myself off and picked up the bike, I was tormented by the lack of empathy, care, or concern. The feeling of being laughed at is perhaps one of the worst feelings any of us can experience. But now that I'm older, I give thanks to that moment and how it's shaped my character. I will laugh with people but never at people. At least not in a condescending way. This experience, among others, has shaped my character. Compassion has me moved to extend my hand when I see someone fall. Always with the intention of assisting them in standing back up."

"Continue to be the asshole that you are, and life will serve to you in exact measure or greater, the same bullshit you dish out to others. Life's punishment is always dealt swiftly. Though you might appear happy and be rich in the world, it is your jail. A low vibrational mindset from which you can never escape."

"If your mind is in a fog and you're a little unclear as to why you are here, let me remind you. You're here to smile, laugh, love and be loved. You're here not only to live, but you're also here to thrive!"

"There are people among us who stand silent, but their presence speaks a thousand words. What does your silence say about you?"

"Walking dead is what we have become. Robbed of our humanity and culture, we fell in tune with the music of the crown and were easily led astray. Enchanted by the music of the Pied Piper and the collective vibration of the crowd, we became hypnotized and disconnected from the rhythms of our own hearts. Unconsciously, we work and live like ants in service to an understanding that's not our own. Our mental and physical sensibilities were corrupted by a virus that has snatched our bodies away. Yet, there's an awakening occurring. There are those of us able to hear the rhythms of our own hearts. We're dancing to a different beat. Fearful of being discovered, we must pretend that we are asleep as we look upon the masses moving strangely. Realizing that the world was changed into a living cemetery and those of us awakened represent those born again."

"Sometimes we must step down to step up. Sometimes we need a moment of pause and deep reflection to remind us of who we were to ignite our fire, launching us into who our Creator meant for us to be."

"Caring is a commodity, whose value is sourced from the heart. Its true value can't be bought or sold. It is something that can only be shared or exchanged. If anybody can put a price tag on it, it ain't real."

"One of our greatest fears is in discovering that someone we have a love for, doesn't love us back. Someone whose attention we desire has no care or concern in equal measure. Unfortunately, at one time or another, we have all experienced this pain. A reality we would rather ignore. Yet, this truth must be confronted. We climb life's ladder without harness. We trust in the event of something going wrong that the person we embrace as a friend will catch us if we slip or fall. However, the truth is awkward and very uncomfortable. How many times have you had a real loved one say, "this person ain't good for you," only to get upset by the stench of the comment or conversation? You convince yourself that no one else truly knows. It is only when you fall do you begin to recall the doubts along life's ladder. The doubts that you ignored. At every step, you remember the harsh words that you easily forgave and dismissed. You remember your every effort to make sure this person was good and how when you were in need, how easily they forgot and didn't show up. Even worse, after you had fallen, they stood along the sidelines without extending a hand to help you up. If you've been fortunate enough to survive one of these relationships, your body lays tattered by the betrayal and flaws of your own judgement.

Rather than be upset and live a life of being wounded without letting anyone in, stop and give thanks for having survived… for graduating and for developing a clearer vision of reality, which has taken you one step closer to being able to discern what is real."

"Why do people take kindness for weakness? Health, wealth, and abundance are not the only things that overflow. Pain, suffering, upset and agony overflow as well. Oftentimes, when a person is overflowing with grief and pain, they look consciously and unconsciously for someone with whom to share it. Kindness is a softness like a sponge, capable of absorbing the spills, while anger is dense and non-porous. Hence, people are drawn to those with whom they can share the weight of their burden. Give thanks for those who are true Alchemists, who can absorb the weight of another, transforming it into something lighter."

"Often, we can't embrace a comfortable feeling because of the damage done to our hearts. We no longer understand or trust its tonal language of love. We no longer have the lived interaction to interpret these heartfelt expressions. Instead, we have grown accustomed to embracing feelings of depression, distrust, not feeling good enough, loneliness, being invisible, unsuccessful, insignificant, or worthless. These feelings are vibratory tones that subdue us. They leave us in a state of being a victim. They imprint pain over our natural compulsion to love. We must learn how to get ourselves clean and how to heal what has been broken so that we can understand the vibratory love language of our hearts. Having successfully done so, we can once again embrace the sensation of feeling upbeat, valued, appreciated, centered, connected, desired, sought after, welcomed, and invited. Letting this language spring forth from our soul into our daily interaction with one another and being fearful no more."

"All of us are challenged with moments where we feel clouded, unable to focus our attention, plan or give concise answers, responses, or directions. Sometimes, we are overwhelmed with a thought so wrenching that we lose our ability to act. Consumed by the moment as though time suddenly stopped. We are forced to embrace our fear and inevitably grow stronger. Even in the midst of this pain, life requires that we give more. Life requires that we give our focus over to a higher power and reflect on life's blessings with gratitude and appreciation finding comfort, come what may."

"Those of us that spend our days concerned about others never want to find ourselves in a position where we fail to act or respond to the needs of our loved ones. Our life missions, results of our own challenges, have us moved to be providers, caretakers, conductors, and saviors of some sort. We want our kindred clan to avoid the pitfalls of life that we have had to dance with. Know that no one can truly save you except you. But along life's journey, it's good to have friendly faces like street signs, naming the path and giving safe direction. There is no greater honor than aiding someone in connecting with their life's purpose, legacy, and spirit. We best honor our failures and defeats by helping others amongst our clan to win and succeed."

"Reflect on your past and discover the hidden messages and meanings in the reoccurring patterns of your life. What is the common character in the people that you pursue and those that pursue you? What circumstances and events, like a scenario from a movie, constantly repeat themselves in your life? What emotion have you married yourself to? Why? If it's fear, how have you allowed it to shape your outcomes? You are the artist of your grand design. Understand your canvas so that you can paint your masterpiece with brighter colors!"

"Our shit is food or fertilizer to something else. Know that everything has value. Just be mindful of the negative value your own shit has to you and the positive value of staying out of other people's shit as well. Unless you're a fly."

"How do we change our reality? We ain't Dorothy in The Wizard of Oz. No glass slippers to click together. No wizard behind the curtain to hear our appeal. No good witches to cast safety spells. All we got is ourselves and maybe one another. Has God ignored our cries? No mothership has dropped from the sky. So, with body, mind, and spirit, we must defend our sovereignty. Perhaps this is our Creator's cry. Either we submit, standstill, or fight! But in the light of night, I, you, and we must choose!"

"For a partnership of any sort to work, it must be equally yoked. Everyone must have something of value at risk. Something of value to share. To have benefits with no equity creates an imbalance that dooms the relationship before it even begins."

"If you're going to measure a person, measure their intention, measure their conviction, and measure their heart. At the end of the day, the substance of all things is born from these spirits."

"The greatest opposition that you'll ever face in life are the voices you hear in your own head. Against this opposition, there's no coveting and there's no hiding. Every fear, like a knife, has a firm grip and a clear bull's eye. But if you dig deep, beyond these shadows, you'll discover the presence of something greater. Keep up the fight so that the real you can emerge."

"When you play someone else's game, you're always on the defense. You're always having to respond or react in a manner that's convenient to someone else's game plan. It's like being attacked in an unfamiliar place. You know not where to run. You have no existing strategy in hand. Caught off guard, you're at the mercy of someone else's intent. Being prepared is exercising your abilities in such a way that regardless of what comes, you're capable of responding in the most efficient way possible under conditions you have not chosen."

"Our habits are practices meant to serve us. A good or bad habit that we make directly correlates with a feeling we seek. Our habits should elevate us, maintain us, and carry us to a safe space but this is not always the case. Instead, our habits deliver us toward satisfaction, which doesn't always serve us. Our goal should be to develop discipline in such a way that our good habits are spontaneous responses to life's events, like a plane on auto pilot."

"A navigation device is programmed to deliver you to your destination. Your destination is usually a feeling or sensation such as sexual gratification, happiness, or even pain. If you're unclear as to what satisfies you, look no further than your habits. They are the signpost. They are also the broken pieces of bread left along life's trail to aid you in returning to the feeling, good or bad, that you have learned through love or trauma to embrace. Hell, it could even be in the coding of your DNA. A gift by God or a map, like evolution, left as a blood memory by your ancestors for your survival. If a habit you have no longer serves your greater good, let it go! Let it go with love!"

"To everything, there is a cycle and a season. Nothing is forever. If we're obedient to these processes, the possibility of our success, longevity, and joy is greater."

"To my conscious collective, born of flesh, blood and bone… we can't ascend our circumstances if we are weighed down by our fears. If we are to create anything great, we must continue to put ourselves at risk. Not blindly but wisely!"

"Despite the coming storm, the daily attacks, and the disconnect from a family l know and know not, I choose to embrace a feeling of love rather than hate. I gravitate to a certain good feeling rather than uncertain speculation. I remain hope-filled toward a day I will not live to see rather than drown myself in these moments of obscurity. Life is endless, but our time in this domain is limited. Staying lit despite our circumstances may be the only real choice we have."

"After being weighed down by life, lightening your heart is a guaranteed way to be lifted."

"Silence is a virtue, often disregarded by those who wish to be seen. Your silence only underscores the power of your presence in such a way that when you do speak, all present bear witness to the power of your voice and the rapture it unleashes."

"Shadows aren't bad. They are the coarseness needed to smooth out our bumpy edges. Like yin and yang, one cannot exist without the other."

"You "getting got" in pursuit of a gain was never the issue. We all must take risk, but your self-centeredness causes you to make uninformed decisions without proper consultation, which lacks not only consideration but shows your willingness to put all those you claim to love at risk! That's why I can't rock with you!"

"In preparation for any new beginning, there are doors we must enter. All that we do in this domain determines our trajectory in another. So, be mindful of what you do in this life. Its implications determine what happens to your spirit in the next life."

"If life requires you to take a life, do so in self-defense or in defense of those you love. There is no power above that will look down upon you."

"Let me be clear that what is most important to me are the people I consider family. More important than money is the currency shared between people I love and so much so that it has me making time even when I don't have it to give."

"Hold on a minute! It's their shit!!!! You are not required to carry other people's luggage, wipe their asses, or nurse their wounds. It's theirs! But all of us, on occasion, get overwhelmed by the stench of what touches us. People who we sometimes hold dear but can't stand, pull us into their condition. And just like day transitioning into night, you find yourself in this position, not knowing how you got there. Emotionally drawn in and held captive by the weight of what pains another's heart."

"Letting go doesn't mean forgetting. It means rising above the grasp of those who would purposely lower you to their level."

"Some people hurl rocks from safe spaces. Intentional acts of violence that are perpetuated by people who never confront you directly. They make up stories in their heads, which they become attached to and never want to hear the truth. Instead, they prefer their lie. Then they use their relatedness to torment you, as if you had an unpaid debt. They intentionally set out to invoke every violent emotion while playing Jenga with their life and yours."

"There is no victory in condemnation. The act itself only reveals the scar one attempts to conceal upon their own reflection."

"Intentionally playing with a person's emotions is a malicious act of violence. It is a predatory form of manipulation, whose scars run deep and usually go undetected."

"What is the obstruction that handicaps your ability to admit guilt when mistakes are made? To err is human and to apologize for a momentary lapse in judgement may not repair the damage done, but it demonstrates to the world that you are indeed human, and it will initiate the closure process for those impacted."

"Cowardice is a momentary disconnect. It is the absence of the Creator's presence. A deflection against a clear conclusion. An avoidance of death at any cost. It is both enemy and friend."

"There will always be some among us that are stronger than others. Those that act as a column, anchor, root, or base, keeping everything else around them alive, well, and together. For these people who allow you to stand, take flight, jump, or dive, give thanks. Your life would not exist without them."

"We must really learn what it means to love one another and let go of this garbage that has us take shots at one another, especially when one acts in accordance with the Creator's purpose in their own existence. If what I do doesn't encumber what God has for you to do, then stay out of my lane. We may aid one another, but you have not the right to infringe on another's right to life."

"We must break away from the status quo and mundane. We must give shape to our own identities and rise to our own processes, practices, customs, mythologies, and methodologies. Life is a sport and it's nearly impossible to win at someone else's game. So, pause for a moment and give thought to a world of your own design that does not reflect any of the flaws and injustices of the container we are in!"

"Always allow love an opportunity to shine through. In situations where you wish to scream, take a breath, and allow your heart's light to shine through. Sharing your concern rather than your anger. Truth be told, when you allow yourself to become enraged, it only reveals your own pain and flaws, which does very little to communicate what's needed to those you love."

"Silly of me to think that anything could ever be mine. All that we ever truly have, we were given at birth. Anything other than that is housed outside of our physical selves as a temporary gift."

"Anything that you give in life comes right back to you. Be mindful what you give. Its forward thrust only increases in velocity as it hurls around the circle of life, like a boomerang, right back to you."

"Interesting how life shapes our intention. At every step of our existence, some form of opposition meets us head on, revealing its ugly head and we are left shaking ours. This engagement reveals us to ourselves and awakens us to our calling."

"Take responsibility for both the fools and devils you attract and allow into your life, never again putting yourself and those you love in harm's way."

"I have heard the witness that has given consent to all of my confusion and the voice is mine! There is no greater enemy than the one within that senses doubts, distrust, and disbelieves in its own vibratory tone, always choosing to follow another's. So, on this day with gratitude and appreciation, I will learn to embrace and give volume to this presence. Never again will I give the audience authority to direct me. No more silent consent. I have awakened my voice and it will no longer allow the enemy within to take charge and I passively consent."

"We've forgotten what it is to take care of one another. We stress over the thought of doing a good deed. We question whether a gesture of goodwill will be properly received. We must overcome our fears of pouring into one another. These divisive sensations give life to demons within. We must put into practice building connection and community again. It is our cleanse. If healing is going to come about, it can only come through this means and not from somewhere without."

"Be the hope and healing that our community needs. Be their source of support. Not just with finances, but with the currency generated by your heart. Performing service and volunteerism simply by listening, sharing a kind word, wearing a smile, or by having a welcoming presence, you change the temperament of the energy around you. Yes, we must be the medicine that each of us needs, for one another."

"Pain and sorrow will always be a part of our psyche. So, rather than be victimized by them, let us forecast the storms that lie ahead and plan our descent. Let us call upon our ancestors and angelic forces while putting our ritual practices to use, so that they can provide protection from the enemy that lies dormant within."

"Don't be so foolish to take on the world without support. It's a battle you will not win. Instead, the true challenge before you is defeating the enemy within by making friends with this sensation inside of you."

"Pain associated with stress doesn't have to be your enemy. It can be your friend. Simply use it as a tool to measure your tolerance level in any area of life. A line of demarcation. An indicator of your strength, which you can increase by exercising your body's ability to engage whatever pressures in life that are before you. Now, what you once considered heavy is light and the only difference is you."

"Every now and again, I find myself compelled to tell someone, "Fuck it" or "Fuck you" before I'm able to graciously settle back into my meditative stance. The power is in the release. It's hurling of energy away from your station, typically toward another. It is a verbal spell of disconnection and on occasion, we smite our intended target with this prayer."

"We treat every painful memory like a flower inside of a bouquet. Its floral fragrance harbors a reminder of a moment we wish we could forget. We'd prefer these memories were like their petals and would simply wither away. Yet, this is how we torture ourselves, concealing our pain in the most beautiful of things."

"An atmosphere of happiness is sustained by being connected to its sensation. It's sort of like being plugged in and having the authority to simply ignite your light with the flick of your switch. Happiness is connected to being lit."

"If what you want people to like most about you is your appearance and you have no concern for how they embrace your heart or intelligence, you simply want to be an accessorized tree that later will be used as mulch, firewood, or fertilizer."

"If in pursuing your dreams you impose upon another who without argument or upset leverages your weight so that you're able to make it safely to the other side, be mindful enough to show appreciation. Nothing hurts worse than carrying the weight of another and then when they make it to safety, not only do they not leave or toss you a line, but they pretend you don't exist."

"If the atmosphere you cultivate is one of happiness, then your environment is never short of goodness."

"What difference does it make that you said it? If it wasn't said with the intention of touching their hearts, then it didn't mean anything. A loving word is empty without the Spirit of Love behind it."

"What happens when our cities are turned to rubble? We learn the cost of our comfort and what we mistook for peace was a temporary patch to what we refused to balance and make whole."

"The memories that we have are sometimes the links in the chain that bind us. Some of us consider it a blessing to have a mental Constitution, where they forget nothing. Yet, they are left grappling with things they are unable to let go of. Then there are those who can recall little to nothing except for a feeling and every day, they get to reset and begin again. To extol the value of one over the other is like comparing whose grass is greener. Each has its hardship and benefit."

"What good is it to smile when what lays hidden behind it is pain? Smile, we must… for the demons that lay in wait hidden around us are looking for the opportunity to feast on the vibration sent from the tension worn on our face, signaling that we're ready to be consumed."

"Those that appear most powerful are truly weak. True power requires no assignment. No wealth, status, or army to lead. These are simply dressings. True power is bare, and lays hidden beneath the skin you're in."

"We can't always forecast the storms before us, nor can we escape natural disasters. But we can be mindful of our concern for one another, allowing love to be a part of our protective gear, come what may."

"Learn to embrace that feel-good moment that you are in and when you feel it waning, don't fear its disappearance. Simply give thanks, igniting its flame again."

"What good are you if your life doesn't touch somebody else's? If you should depart tomorrow, what statement will your life have made on those around you? Be clear that you can be foe, friend or an empty vessel passing in the wind. How would you like to be remembered?"

"Allow love a place to live. All of us have experienced loss, rejection, and hate. For some, those experiences have formed memories within us that we wish we could forget. They've given shape to the containers we've become… shallow, dense, and unable to let love in. If you could release the trauma of those experiences, would you? Would you soften the skin you're in? We are simply clay and when baptized by water, it hydrates the body and moistens our skin, allowing our bodies to stretch and breathe. We lose weight and lighten ourselves. We take on a new shape. We breathe in our blessings and exhale our pain allowing love a space to be."

"What is freedom, in this domain, without discipline and sacrifice? All of us are required to make investments of time and energy into the development of our bodies' physical wellness and cognitive function. Our learning gives interpretation to our intuitive spirit and soul's assigned mission. We decipher our calling by tuning our container in such a way that it's able to interpret our Creator's directives directly. Thus, aiding us in navigating the terrain of this physical existence."

"Gratitude should come from birth, but depending on your point of entry, embracing this life could be like landing in the fires of hell. It's only after you survive without getting burnt that you realize that the difficulties placed before you were trials meant to aid you in your becoming."

"Victory is neither in winning nor losing. It's the ability of summoning and keeping God's presence throughout the fight!"

"You discover who people are not in the light of day, but in the darkness of night. I've seen the brightest people go dark in moments of difficulty and conflict. Truth is that there is a vampire in all of us and unfortunately with most, it doesn't require much of a conflict to bring it out."

"Along this journey of life, I've lost some good friends. Not from death but from the crossroads of life where we got separated. Separated by our misunderstandings, egos, insecurities, and simple stuff that, at the time, seemed as massive as Mount Everest. I give thanks for these people who, in some form or fashion, were my mirrors that helped me to discover myself. These are the people I pray for. Those, who in moments of confusion and growth, took the time to give me both light and air! They were my true teachers."

"Sometimes, it takes a moment to get rid of the stains of life. For some, a moment can last a lifetime. But if you put in the work and are fortunate to discover life as a teacher and friend, then perhaps what you in your past has measured as misfortune, you may now understand as being your blessings."

"Without the challenges of life, we cannot grow. The greatest riches cannot be held in your hands. They must be felt by your soul."

"Many of us spend our days crying and "boo-hooing", afraid of letting go of what pains us. Hoping that somehow, something or someone will come and save us. The riddle before us is ourselves. We'd rather kill ourselves than face ourselves. We'd rather hold on to what pains us rather than risk it on a feeling of happiness that evades us. Our only resolve at awakening goodness within us is to rely on outside stimuli to access goodness that we've buried deep inside. Center yourself, be gentle with yourself, and allow love to cleanse your battered soul so that the light within you can glow, needing no assistance."

"We are all looking for someone else to be responsible for a decision we must make. Whatever your decision or direction, go with God!"

"This fantasy, false reality, and matrix is simply a self-contained prison that has us unable to truly connect, touch, hear, see, or love. Instead, we live a reality attempting to escape our fears. Unfortunately, there is no freedom in always playing it safe. When you do so, what you live is death."

"We must each write the story of our own becoming. If not, we become simple actors in the unfolding saga of someone else's thoughts. We, too, have the capacity to create and narrate. Let us be authors of our circumstances and collaborators in the creation of the world in which we live."

"We need to build on the concept that less is more. Our society is lifestyle driven. They are preoccupied with the notion that to be important, you must have more. All we are, are slaves to plenty. We thirst for more, not knowing the weight of what we crave truly makes us less."

"Hope diminishes as time expires. Confronting this truth has us teary-eyed and upset. No one wants to lose hope but if death be near, live! Embrace every moment and every breath. Hope is simply your reminder to stay lit."

"Your hate only exposes your own sickness. Refuse to succumb to this virus. Its sensation is all-consuming. Hate is the one thing we learn to love, which lowers our vibration."

"Life always creates opportunities for us to discover what we value most, only to have us struggle between what our heart desires and what we've been taught is most important for our survival. The daily saga between our head and our heart. Choose wisely, as life demands ignoring one intelligence over the other. But if we're meant to succeed, we must marry these two witnesses from within. Their union gives birth to power, passion, and purpose, letting us know that our lives are about more than just our survival. We are God-sent."

"Sometimes it takes a moment to remove the stains of life. For some, a moment can last a lifetime. For others, a moment is a few days, hours, minutes, or seconds. Whatever the case, the shit before us is fertilizer to help us grow."

"Fearful of our positioning and any shifts that might have us suffer a loss, we cling to our situations as if holding on to the edge of a ledge. Fearful of falling, we make no attempt to climb to safety. We just hug the wall for dear life. Unbeknownst to us, true freedom is simply a movement away. All we are required to do is trust ourselves and let go."

"Give no thought to what you don't want in your life. Don't make the mistake of becoming like the streetlight in the night. A beacon giving invitation to all sorts of demons to come consume the heat from your light."

"Some of us are directed, and we move with the wind. Others of us find motivation only in the grind. We only awaken to go against the flow of things. Whatever your calling, whether it be to cast a sail or move against a current, know what powers you and move accordingly."

"How great is it to have people that love you so much, that they become the sowers of mischief, the carriers of disease, writers on the wall of your life, who unintentionally in their writings press so hard that they leave scars… all because you've given them access. But welcome them you must because they are love's lens and through them, you can clearly see the true source of your problems. The ones you would otherwise ignore. They are often the "carriers" and not the "cold". We all share life's journey together. These moments are simply a part of life's ebb and flow. Often, they are moments that lead us to anger, but appreciate them you must because God is at work. Working through you and others to reveal what is concealed, elevating us in the creation of His Grand Design. We are in a space and time where information is abundant. Yet everyone feels as though they need to learn more in order to grow and be successful. It's my contention that more information isn't what's needed. Perhaps we need to mine our own minds and figure out ways to dispose of harmful beliefs, inner struggles, and self-dialogues that inhibit our progression toward our own wellness, freedom, and success."

"Fear is a sensation that nudges us on our shoulders and wraps itself around our minds. A stimulant alerting us to dangers that are perceived or real. Yet, whether real or not, it is a warning. A call to arms. A moment to find shelter or armor up for whatever is to come. Self-protection is the rule. Understanding "self" as family and community is the goal. We are truly all we got. Fear is a necessary emotional response. Yet, when sustained, it becomes a poison. It is the venom we pump into our own veins when not properly dispensed into the perceived threat. It hardens and becomes the thorn in our backside. It is the witness within us that comes to alert us. A friend that we smother and hold onto, making it into our enemy instead."

"It's not always that we have a plan in place but, we are required to operate from an intention with everything we do at this moment. Handle what stands before you in the present and the future will align and tend to itself accordingly."

"In the midst of battle, we need to focus our attention keenly on the sensation that holds us together and not the source of division that is attempting to break us apart. This intention is your armor."

"Engage a person for what they know and not for what they don't know. Stop your judging and put your prejudice aside. Look beyond what's visible to your eyes and discover the gifts that stand before you. You'd be surprised how your Creator, whom you curse, has given you all you need and not only to survive but thrive."

"If you have a habit, daily practice, ritual, or routine that no longer serves you, let it go. You are the engineer and architect of the domain you are in. Structure and prepare for yourself what allows you to rest warmly in the sunset and has you bright-eyed and excited in the early dawn to commence your day strong. You are an instrument of love, crafted by our Creator. Discover your tone and sing your own melodies and song. Bringing with it harmony and flow that allows us each a space to shine and grow."

"Wanting success without failure is like wanting to swim without water. To think you can roll out a red carpet to your destination without pause is ludicrous."

"What's most broken about us isn't our hearts. It's everything else about us. Our hearts have kept us together and keep us from falling completely apart. If we mend some of our other broken parts, the heart's intelligence will not only keep us from falling apart but will initiate healing that will have us stand up."

"Be a voice of reason in such a way that when someone hears your voice, it compels them out of their darkness into the light that has always stood before them."

"Let your voice resonate a frequency of peace, love, and comfort in such a way that when your people hear you, it compels them out of their darkness. Stay lit!"

"When what's most broken about you weighs you down and feels like it can't be fixed, give thanks! Give thanks for the days when you were strong and when whatever now straggles about you fit tight and worked right. Give thanks for the body, which has housed and given you shelter and carried you in directions that you ought to go. Give thanks for its service because when you part ways, it cannot come. It must return to the Earth in the same way you must return back to the Sun. Give thanks!"

"We all fall short from time to time and get lost measuring the distance left behind. Although we may not have far to go, getting stuck on past memories will slow, if not stop your flow. We get lost in our memories of days past. Yes, we took for granted these moments that we had."

"Now the challenge before us is to take a moment to stand, turn, be still, and take a helping hand. The sign before you that you once could not see is a signal of your victory. Push through!"

"If how you perceive me is as a threat, then you have every right to keep your distance and stay away. In doing so, you do us both a favor. I don't hold space with people I do not love and cannot trust."

"We are all like algebraic characters- expressions of symbols, representing purpose and meaning. We are not mistakes. We are Creator sent. Yet, upon our arrival in this domain, we lose our connection to autopilot, and we surf this domain manually. Here is where we have a choice. So, choose wisely. You can be a variable in life or a constant. Should we choose the latter, our presence brings order to the universe, allowing variables to discover their true purpose as constants. Remember!!!"

"The stains and stench of life are what grab us. Sometimes people identify too much with the shit they are in and become it. Most times, people just happen to step in it. Unbeknownst to them, they move about, not realizing what stains and pains them. It's not until they see the flies that they attract do they realize what they've become and the need to get clean."

"You're the application being programmed. Your device has limitations, based on its design. Your output correlates with your input. If garbage is what you pour into it, what expectation do you have about what you get out of it? Unless you're a practitioner of alchemy, garbage in will always equal garbage out."

"When something you want is evading you, summon what it is that you want and then lean into it. You're both the needle and the thread. When you are clear about your direction, remove yourself from your shelter and lean into what it is that you want in such a way that you can feel the wind pierce your skin. Know your tip. Let it gain entry as you guide the point. This is no simple task. Sometimes you have got to lancet life and draw blood from it in order to capture the design that lays hidden before you. So, whether you're tasting it, smelling it, appreciating it, simply lean into it. It is the object of your desire. When what has evaded you can no longer run, hold still, and ask for it to come. Exercise your real strength. Create your own reality and make life come toward you as you lean into it."

"Whatever commands our attention controls our focus and controls us. It is both our weakness and strength. It is the food we consume that either nourishes or poisons our minds and impacts our every decision. If we want to free ourselves, let us curve our attention and be more selective over what thoughts that we allow entry into the precious womb of our minds."

"You don't always want people to engage you when they think you're good. You want to see how people engage you when they believe you're hurt or wounded. You'd be surprised to discover the buzzards, wolves, and bears scattered among those that you thought had love for you. Some are there just for the feeding and when you have nothing else for them to consume, they will attempt to consume you."

"When what you seek evades you and you can no longer run, hold still, stay steady, and ask for it to come. Your power is in your presence, lightness, and stillness. It's being grounded. It's here that you discover what you've been seeking. If you had not been chasing, there would be no need for it to run. Simply work on being a better you, invite success into your life, and watch it come."

"It's unfortunate that we live in a system that has us distrustful of ourselves and one another but distrust we must. Until someone has earned your trust, exercise caution before giving it freely. Don't even fully trust yourself until you've been properly grounded, removing the enemy from within."

"Uncertainty has us having to make the right decision for everyone else which has us handicapped, at times, from directing ourselves. It's like putting a right shoe on a left foot. It's simply doesn't fit. It's uncomfortable. Yet, life continues to move and doesn't stop. There is no time to pause. Day in and day out, we are tasked with having to make the same decisions for ourselves as we make for others. We forget how to place ourselves at center stage. Hell, we forget how to place ourselves on the stage. Suddenly, everything in life is a reaction that demands our attention. No time to ponder other possibilities. Our lives are consumed, and we're left wondering… how in the hell did we arrive here?"

"Stop clinging to your upsets. Discover the inclination that gives you permission to let them go. After their release, you may feel the dawning of a sensation of happiness that you need to feed with the same intensity as what weighed you down."

"I don't trust the others any more than they trust us. It's stupid to think that people who have done so much to harm the world would ever want to have us as their masters. It's only through this lens that they see us. Behind their fear is a belief that we are more than their equal."

"I don't think like you. I don't process things the way that you do. I don't move the way that you do. If I did, I'd be you. Be mindful of the expectations that you place on others. People may be similar, but no one is the same. People will either fall short, rise up, or discover their own direction by the measure of the expectations you have of them. At days end, we must respect each other's sovereignty, despite disliking our inability to control the limbs that are not our own."

"There is a cost to living. Some of us seem to be taxed more than others. Yet, our payments are the same. Oxygen in and carbon dioxide out is the exchange. We pay with every breath. Without this agreement, life for us would not exist. Yet, there are those who espouse to be believers in God and yet ignore this simple law of life, polluting the air we share. Our beliefs will always be measured against our actions, allowing us to discern who's real and who's not."

"Some of us don't discover our connections until we stand in moments of crisis. Then, all the fluff and pageantry disappear. What kept us at a distance seems to shrink away, taking with it all of what pained us. Embrace the opportunity to forgive and be forgiven. Like snakes, we too can grow new skin and shed the old. Awakening from our entanglement aligned and complete."

"Had we not gone through life's difficulties, there would be no way of measuring the value of the blessing before us. What you thought was a difficulty was actually a gift. Had you not been disconnected and corralled into a suspicious, fear-filled thought, you'd be basking in the blessings of our Savior, who you blindly search for outside of yourself, never realizing our Savior's residence exist in each of us."

"Life is a seesaw played best when you stand in the center. Here is where you can find balance. Balance is power. Here is where you discover how to flow, riding the ups and downs… while the masses occupy the ends, weighed down by their beliefs."

"Why do people want what you don't have to give? It's almost like the Ancestors are working through others, demanding that you grow and expand to discover your untapped capabilities and gifts. Now, the real question becomes this: why do we resist?"

"Late in life, I was taught to empty my emotional container of worry, regret, upset, and anger to maintain my emotional wellness. But you can't empty your cup if you're drowning in it. You can't empty your cup if you're under water."

"Life without discipline equals death. Short story: While the family and I were vacationing, a good friend house sat for us. While there, he fed our fish. Not knowing the proper amount, he overfed them. When we returned, the fish tank was cloudy and the fish swam back and forth, eating the food until they were dead. Likewise, you may wish for wealth but if you have no discipline, you too, will consume yourself to death."

"Those of you that live in your head and have closed and locked the door to your heart may think yourself smart. But there is a danger that awaits when your ego silences the heart and runs rogue. The head looks for safety while the heart looks for victory. You cannot win at living if your head denies your heart from being."

"Somewhat heavy in my emotions, I find myself falling and unable to smile, laugh or be loving. Fortunately, for me, the observer, when awakened within me, guides me home to a happier space."

"You could be smack dab in the middle of summer and it feels like winter all around. Afraid to smile and you silence the look on your face. You must remain stoic. God forbid these vultures sense any sign of life gleaming from your being. Like flies, drawn to light at night or the walking dead. When they sense life, all will attempt to consume you and consume your brightness. How long must we remain hidden? How long must we cover ourselves, concealing the fire inside us?"

"It saddens me to see those that I love unable to recognize when they're drowning. Deeply submerged beneath dense, cloudy water and weighed down by their fears. Weighed down by iron shackles that they cleverly reimagine as gold. This is the lie they tell themselves, so they don't have to fight the good fight and they choose a rather purposeless life."

"Everyone seems to act as though they arrived here unaided, as though no one else played a significant part in their being, becoming, and survival. Foolish we are to believe that anyone can survive in this world unaided and apart from one another. Likewise, even in the absence of a hand up, one still remains informed that they have to engage this part of life connected to something greater. Having this understanding empowers us to embrace this greatness within us and confront the challenges before us alone."

"When goodness finds its way into the world, some among us do their best to kill it's presence. Like swatting a fly, our distrust of one another and anything spiritual, displaying kindness, warmth, or affection has us questioning and doubting whether these intentions and sensations are real. This very act drains the life force out of the medicine our Creator has birthed into this word and deed. Then we foolishly lash out, questioning our Creator while we ignore its every presence."

"The goal of life is to create heaven in hell. When you're in hell on Earth, you need framework, structures, and systems to service and protect you. Yet, in the midst of the hell you are in, you have to create your own heaven and a space of peace on Earth. This heaven on Earth has barriers and walls. Once you've earned access, there are no locks and doors. There's this sense of freedom within. Yet, after gaining entry, please know you're still surrounded by hell. You've just found your comfortable safe space within your surroundings."

"We give the best of ourselves to feed the beast outside of us and when our days are numbered with fewer days before us, we have no time, desire, or discipline to feed the master within us."

"Courage requires that we face some of our demons alone. But before we enter these battles, we should seek wise counsel. Sharpening our insight brightens our internal light. This preparation is key if we are to find victory."

"How many of you develop anxiety when called upon to stretch yourself but instead, you stress yourself? You get scared to look into the eyes of another, especially your sister or brother because you think that they'll see your every hidden shadow of shame and discover your brokenness and disown, dismiss, and dislike you for cause, as you struggle to discard the shattered shards of glass from your past. Yet, you fail to recognize in your over analyzing and self-consumption that all of us, and I mean all of us, have the same thing in common: we're all broke or have been broken."

"Each of us has a covenant with our Creator. Each of us was created with intention and purpose. All of us are drawn to people who represent threads inside of the containers we're called to create. Our action or inaction in response to our Creator's call will either strengthen or weaken us. Come, we must. It is the pathway to our safety. A summoning we can no longer dismiss or ignore. We are our Creator's answer to the problems before us."

"They want us to be strung out and not strong. They don't want us to be independent and connected but beaten and broken. Against this enemy, we should already be defeated, but something within us compels us to push on. Yes, we are strongly connected, undefeated, and reborn."

"I know the hell we're in and the heaven in this hell that I wish to create. Rules, laws, and boundaries are needed when people can't just be. We must create to regulate and protect the space. I understand the necessity of creating rules and boundaries to safeguard the space I wish to create. However, I wish to create a space where my every window doesn't have bars and my every door doesn't have locks and where access requires that you resonate on entry. It requires an elevated frequency."

"Hell might be us left behind. Our living should be in preparation for our departure. Yet, there are those uncertain of transition and fight to hold on to what they know. Perhaps our punishment in death comes in having failed at life. Fearful and afraid of living, we are forced again to repeat it. To remain in this low vibrational existence, where we only believe and attach ourselves to what we can touch."

"Be able to map out your blessings in the same way that you do your upsets! All of us can find our way to an upset with our eyes closed and then ignore every righteous sign giving us blessed assurance of good to come. We can see demons but ignore every sign of an angel. If you believe in everything bad, take a moment to believe in at least one thing good."

"When people are trying to get their needs met, they will call you without pause. They will promise you the world and they will come with a kind tongue and friendly grin. Once you meet their needs, they will ghost you as if you never existed. Give thanks for this intrusion. Life simply revealed to you the beauty of a flower whose stem was full of thorns. Not everything that seems attractive needs to be touched."

"Doubt and fear have sunken many dreams. They will kill a vessel before it is even built. Let go of this toxin. Your strength is in your knowing and belief. If you've been victimized by these spirit teachers and if they have robbed your air of oxygen, kindly give thanks to their presence before letting them go. Don't wobble in defeat. Consider any losses a tax. Laugh and give thanks for the lesson learned and push forward toward the bounty of blessings that lay before you."

"The higher you are in one reality, the lower you are in another. No wonder we struggle for what we perceive to be a success. Unbeknownst to us, we're fighting against our spirits that have anchored us from moving into a reality it does not want us to fully enter. Yes, what we perceive as success in this domain is death to our spirit in another. So, contemplate your pursuits and be mindful of the cost of entry to where you wish to go."

"Sometimes we lean so far to the right that we end up on our left. Our strong sense of being right has us wrong. There is an inherent danger in believing and at some point, our beliefs get tested. Our sensibilities get tested and we're left either holding on to something we've invested a lifetime believing or we begin to question and examine the contradictions as we navigate life's terrain, searching for what we know and realize to be true."

"There are a lot of fractured people walking the world that don't know they're fractured. Living within their own nightmares. Unable to feel, see, or comprehend anything outside of the realm of their own limited experience and understanding. Be mindful of these people. They are our sisters and brothers but just unaware of their imbalance. Hell, it could be us. Just woke in one regard and sleep in another."

"Sometimes we discover our strengths, not in knowing what we are but in knowing what we're not. It's what happens when a doctor is performing a medical procedure and they're required to remove a cancer. They sever the cords to whatever it's attaching itself to. In cutting the cancer out, what we hope remains is what's healthy. We too must have the skills of a physician and be able to cut the cords to whatever cancers have attached themselves to our bodies. We must be able to maneuver through and around the superfluous details of our lives, letting go of whatever weighs us down and drains us of our life force."

2 WORDS OF ENCOURAGEMENT

"You can't see that you traverse life's upward slope as though there was no elevation at all. You don't recognize the awkward pounding of your heart because its rapid pulse has drummed that same beat since your conception. If not for your rugged determination, you would not exist. Your life being is the story of what trophies actually are. Moments of awe!"

"This world may not embrace you but if love fills your heart and you move with good intent, embrace yourself. You are God-sent. Your presence is the medicine needed for brighter days to come. You are what's right with the world amidst all the chaos."

"Don't let anyone douse your fire. Not anyone! There are those who are so closely connected to you, whom you have no defense against… who, with word, gesture, or act can suffocate your flame. If you can't separate yourself from these people, you must develop your ability to ground yourself so that their negative energy passes through you. Being grounded is your safety."

"I know you spend your days trying to fix yourself to be presentable before the world but please know that despite having been battered by life, you're not broken!"

"We are here to build on a culture of love, care, and concern for the wellness of the world standing before us. So, let's make sure we stay lit and ignite someone else's fire, causing them to smile and have a bright and beautiful day. Our goal is to be like the bees and spread love."

"Man, shit happens to all of us. It's no excuse to stop unless it's simply to gather yourself, rest yourself, build yourself, feed yourself or love yourself. As long as you have breath, you are still required to push through!"

"We all got reason to complain and give up. But what if the reason God has you here is so that you can find answers and solutions to the problems before you? Stop exhausting your energy by complaining. Get focused, get clean, gear up, and push through!"

"Everyone needs at least one person they can say anything to. Therapist, willing family member, or true friend. Regardless of the risk, there are moments when the weight of what we carry must be shared."

"There is no safety in playing it safe. We are all connected in some form or fashion and when one falls, we all are left holding the rope. Life's a team sport and whether you like it or not, you're in the game. My suggestion is for you to choose a team, get your head in the game, and play your position!"

"The most powerful gift we can give one another is an ear! The pathway to our healing lies in our listening. Listening intently, indiscriminately, and completely. Creating a clearing that allows the weight of what we carry to be released to the ethers with love, compassion, and forgiveness. Once achieved, one recognizes an immediate shift of feeling, weight, and disposition, which now must be nourished with the proper practices of care, thoughtfulness, and concern."

"Today is what you make out of it. So, appreciate whatever you have before you and if you're standing there empty-handed with nothing at all, breathe deep and appreciate the air."

"We are not random. Life brings forth what is needed. We are born for a particular purpose with a particular mission. Rediscover the light you are! Remember!"

"Now that you've touched the sky, make your high your new low so that when you stand, the storms of life fall beneath you."

"Though empty-handed, never underestimate your value. You are the gift that keeps giving. Your presence fills the room. Your smile, loving gestures, tight hugs, and warm embrace are the fuel used to awaken the Sun. Your being ignites our flames and diminishes what pains us. You are a happy thought and for you, the fires of life. Give thanks!"

"What you see in your life may be your choice. Even as death stands before you, the beauty of life stands even more near. All stands before you and yet your mind's eye chooses to embrace every painful picture while you ignore every comforting thought, as if mentally and emotionally blocked. Know that even in the midst of terror, your power and armor is in your ability to smile and hold onto a happy thought."

"Every child represents an answer to a question we put before our Creator. We just have to be patient for the response to mature."

"Discover what moves your heart to laugh and smile. Make this your daily muse."

"We always know what our child is thinking because she's not afraid to share her thoughts. Although there are times where I may want to pop her in her mouth, I pause and laugh on the inside because she is exactly the way I want her to be. Strong and sovereign in her beliefs."

"Hate is not a sustainable source of energy. Instead, give yourself a hug every few days in between and consider opting out for this renewable source of fuel to power your heart."

"Pause and give thanks to the Creator's presence that shines bright inside of you. Despite your blemishes, know that what's most beautiful about you is more than skin deep."

"Just because it's not visible, doesn't mean it's not real. Its deliverance into the world will be through you!"

"Trust what is inside you. No one knows the source of your light until you walk through darkness and the glare of comfort and peace illuminates from your presence."

"Your being is essential. So, continue to shine bright! Your presence dispels the darkness. You are a star in my night."

"Push past the fogginess that clogs your mind. Be bold. It doesn't matter that being on the mountain peak places you on all sides of the mountain's edge. Here is where you stand fearful of falling even when our Creator made you to fly."

"Stand up out of misery. Wipe yourself off from defeat. Relax your muscles from the stresses of life that squeeze so tight. We are more than the things we pursue and more than the temples we call our bodies. We are divine light. So, in all that you do, be present to your greatness and shine bright."

"Uplift yourself when there are no visible hands to help you. You'd be surprised the powers you command and the Spirits you can summon to assist you through."

"Step into your darkness to discover your own light."

"No one can hold you more accountable than yourself. Stop beating yourself over the head. Stop your judgement, whether you are to blame or not. To error is to be human. To make amends and correct your errors is to be a man or woman."

"Lighten up! The process of becoming is incremental. It doesn't always occur in a day."

"The process of improving oneself is an unending stairwell with many plateaus."

"We all need life experience in order to appreciate the moment we are in."

"Become preoccupied with the process and stop beating yourself up when you don't reach your expected results. Discipline, focus, and flow become your rewards, outweighing your desired outcome. Once you've mastered the process, you will always be able to achieve your desired results."

"Lessons in life cannot be learned without making mistakes. Be gentle with yourself and try again."

"Please rest. The brightness of your aura, even when you slumber, gives guidance and direction to those connected to your light."

"Being strong for yourself allows you to be strong for others. So always take a moment to fuel your own fire."

"The power of who we are is fueled by our inward smile. Regardless of your situation, condition, or position, continue to love and embrace the Spirit that is you."

"Life is an intuitive process. Trust your gut."

"If you must release yourself from a relationship, don't create an upset to separate. It's okay. Let go with love!"

"Don't be fearful during your descent into darkness. You might discover our Creator's likeness in you. Shine bright!"

"Stop your complaining. We are where we are when we are so that we may grow. Don't get upset because you believe you should be someplace other than where you presently stand. If you have visions of being someplace grand, then make two dots. One dot being where you stand and the other where you wish to go. Simply draw a line connecting the points and get to work toward manifesting your vision. No guarantee that you'll succeed but standing still and complaining won't get you there."

"Truth be told, many of us are married to our feelings of regret, loneliness, anxiety, fear, embarrassment, and depression. Once wed, it's hard to let go but, in order to truly live, we must. Have a fling with gratitude, happiness, self-care, and joy. Then maybe you can find the strength to divorce yourself from what pains you."

"Every day is an opportunity to start anew. So, plan and program. Don't wait for an upset to compel you to move and do what your head and heart ignores and yet knows to be true."

"The stress you bring to a situation is the sickness that consumes you. Control your temperament. Stay lit and shine bright!"

"Many people run to religion to find safety from their desires, not realizing that everyone else they were hiding from ran and sought sanctuary in the same space."

"Slow down, stop your running, pause, pace yourself and catch your breath. Stop chasing what you should attract! Your constant pursuit gives rise to an energy that does more to repel than attract. Find your rhythm and find your flow. Stay centered in your divine frequency and watch all that is yours in the world create a path to your door."

"There are some people driven toward their goals and others that require opposition. The fun for them is in the fight. Yet there are still others who, with prayer and meditation, attempt to summon into being what is needed to manifest into existence their visions. Whatever the process, choose what works for you and push through. Whatever your path, carry your light!"

"Through your own darkness, light will emerge. For this, give thanks!"

"Setbacks give invitation for negativity to come in. It's at this point that you remain firm in your conviction and firm in your vision. These hurdles before you are not meant to stop you but only to increase your ability to leap higher."

"I acknowledge and praise you for keeping up the good fight! I acknowledge and praise you for trying to live a good life. I acknowledge and praise you for holding your head high. I acknowledge and praise you for drowning out their lies. I acknowledge and praise you for pushing through each day. I acknowledge and praise you."

"The hole that you fell in is the same hole you have to climb out. It's easy to fall in and requires a lot of time, focus, and strength to climb out. My advice is to avoid the holes."

"Let go of your fears and lean into life. Feel the wind pierce your skin. This sensation may have you believe you're falling but it is here you discover how to fly."

"When what you seek is just beyond your reach, stretch! You'd be surprised how many people miss out on their success because they are fearful of life's test. Loosen up. Victory is within your reach."

"We have all messed something up one time or another. None of us are perfect. We have all made mistakes. We all have room for growth. Give space for errors. Make space for loss. Lighten up! It only means we're human. How great is that?"

"Thank you for helping me to sprout fully, stand erect, and not bent, and to know the sensation of joy in my heart again."

"Everybody has the wisdom to contribute to the mix. Whatever your gift, be intentional, share, and multiply it. The act of sharing fortifies your own understanding while inviting our Creator's presence into the exchange. Consider this knowing your reward, blessing, and gift."

"As you look in the mirror, be gentle to the figure before you. Stop abusing yourself. Stop doubting yourself. The "you" that you see needs your love, kindness, and forgiveness. You are Co-Creator of the vessel you are in. There is no flaw in your design. Be grateful and allow your light to shine."

"We can't be good for others if we are not good for ourselves. As you make space for others, make sure you make space for yourself."

"If you want to brighten your day, be the Sun. You make the day."

"You're not heavy. So, for a time, allow me to carry you and should you find yourself weighed down, it will be because you found your strength and decided to place me on your shoulders for a time. Doing as Gods do… carry one another."

"Good days are what we make them! Be bright, shinning your light through your upsets and disappointments. Let happiness and being joy-filled rule your day. And when your demons you've grown comfortable with come knocking, deny them entry. Know that it's your hand that opens the gates to your hell, giving access to what enters. You do not deserve the abuse you've consented to. Let your strength be in self-forgiveness and understanding the proper use of the word 'no.' For this we give thanks!"

"If fear of dying has you not living, consider yourself already among the dead. Dismay and procrastination will not serve you. Wake up to the reality of your calling. Embrace your assignment, stay lit, and do your work."

"Whatever you consume, consumes you. Every thought, vibration, inclination, and intention. Be mindful of what you consume. Let every thirst, addiction, craving, inclination, and conviction be of something good that feeds and elevates your heart, mind, and spirit. Be joy filled."

"Know that a well-balanced diet in this domain is needed. Consume more joy, wellness, appreciation, gratitude, fortitude, self-forgiveness, and bliss for a healthier, wealthier life."

STAY LIT BY DARNELL P. SMITH

3 FOOD FOR THOUGHT

STAY LIT BY DARNELL P. SMITH

"There are those among us who are weighed down by the silver they collected from the people they have betrayed and killed. Yes, it is a bounty that will afford them an opportunity to escape the slums occupied by those of us once considered family but, the stench of death follows them and keeps their spirit captive to an eternity in purgatory, which they so gleefully smile and consider heaven."

"There are two types of cemeteries- those that are well-maintained and those where weeds are allowed to run wild. But whether manicured or wild, what remains the same is that the dead are dead, and spirits of the dead no longer make their home there. Feed from the richness of what has passed!"

"We take shots at people that extend us a hand and give a pass to those who give us no thought at all."

"Unfortunately, the art of communication has been lost. Rather than talk to one another, we talk at one another. We actually engage in battles every day, without physical blows ever being thrown. We have become skilled at the art of domination and manipulation but know nothing of building or exchanging. Instead, we perform war rituals. We dance in conversation, flexing our style and strength while any real opportunity for growth gets lost."

"There are those among us that think they have ascended to the heavens but unbeknownst to them, their heads are simply lost in the clouds."

"Sometimes we find happiness in the simplest of things. It could be knitting, swimming, coloring, singing, or skateboarding. Yet there are those of us who would work and amass wealth but never imagine or feel the happiness experienced by those doing these simple things."

"If the space you occupy is one of constantly playing it safe, then you might discover later in life that the success you desired stood just outside the door you feared to enter."

"Stop opening the door for misery. It cannot gain entry without your consent."

"Regardless of your circumstance, gratitude is a well that should never run dry!"

"Know your power from where you stand. It starts with whatever you can touch and spirals forward."

"If what you value most in life has a dollar sign attached to it, then you value nothing."

"The biggest mountains you may ever shift are in your mind."

"Once the enemy has you, the concern isn't any longer about dropping the soap. It's whether or not you bend down or squat to get it."

"Don't allow what's been planted in your head to usurp authority and go against the other intelligence in your body. Don't ignore what raises your hair and causes your heart to flutter. Sometimes what you fear is real."

"I can measure my value based on whether or not a person answers my call. Or when they miss it, how long it takes them to call me back, if at all. Nothing for me to address or correct. Just keeping a mental note. And if you should call me, you'd learn the same."

"Everyone acts as though Halloween is once a year when people are walking around in masks and costumes every day."

"Be mindful of fools, but don't give them your full attention. If you do so, you risk becoming a fool, too. Life will lower you to their level just so you can understand them."

"I could scream fire, but it wouldn't matter. Everyone is already consumed by all the smoke."

"I do not want to debate about it. I want to build on it. Maybe one day our community might learn this difference."

"What happens when the terror we impose on the rest of the world begins knocking at our door?

"Understand where you stand. Every container has its own special set of rules."

"Our existence is evidence that all the fires of hell don't burn."

"It's alright to keep things buried away but please be aware whatever you bury will bring forth new life, increasing in greater measure whatever you attempt to conceal."

"We all have darkness that envelops us, that grabs at us, and that mirrors itself in people that we do not wish to see. Living in fear of the moment when someone shines a light on the shadows of our past. But don't be alarmed. You are not alone. Know that in the closet of darkness, beside your shit sits the shit of the person casting a light on you. Had it not been for the stench of their own shit, they wouldn't see yours."

"Everybody is in service to something. All of us have something within us that needs to be fed. What does the hunger in you have you gravitate to?"

"Sometimes we're too quick to reach a conclusion before we have fully examined all angles of an issue. Sometimes in order to overstand the wisdom of a decision, we must allow things to unfold."

"Twenty years of watching someone shovel shit doesn't inspire you to want to be a better shit shoveler. It's quite the opposite. It has you exercise your mind in such a way that you never want to use a shovel!"

"We all fall into holes. It's just that some people's holes are deeper than others."

"You cannot say you have atoned when you have not attempted to make amends to those you've offended or harmed!"

"Our world appears to be dying because those who are called will not come!"

"Why the wall? Because all that comes cannot enter. Each of us is medicine for another. Just be mindful of the handful that are medicine for you."

"If the atmosphere you create or cultivate is one of happiness, then your environment is never short of goodness."

"If the sensation of hunger has you, you should know that whatever you crave is what you've made into your God."

"Change is never discretionary. It will occur with or without you."

"Betrayal has its own rewards. With it may come riches but at a cost. A spiritual bounty that weighs you down with fear, making you the camel that God couldn't thread through an eye of a needle."

"To jar oneself from the routines of life requires that we do something different, if not extreme."

"Everybody concerned about appearances, but don't nobody give a "f" about substance."

"Interdependency is part of the human experience. It's foolish to think that living can be done alone."

"It's amazing how we can do so much for others but so little for ourselves. Unfortunately, unbeknownst to most, the work we do for others is actually us working on ourselves."

"If you ever find yourself in a sunken space, finding something to be grateful for is the rope left behind to help you climb out."

"Self-preservation can be an illness, especially if it has you ready to destroy the world just to save yourself."

"A slave is not a servant, and a servant is not a slave. Those who assume positions of service willfully are royalty."

"True wisdom is conferred when what you once measured as misfortune is what you now understand as being your blessing instead."

"When all hope diminishes and our time together here seems to be nearing an end, answer this one question: would you do it over, if you could do it all again?"

"We must discover the beauty of the road taken and stop glancing over our shoulders, wondering if we chose the right direction."

"It might serve you to adjust your vision or position when looking at what you think might be a loss. Sometimes a victory comes in a defeat."

"If winning is a mindset, then victory can be found in defeat."

"One might think these are perilous times. Our world is not ending. Just evolving into what remains to be seen."

"Have you ever had anyone who turned from day to night on you? In a moment, almost as if someone or something clouded or shaped their judgement? Then they speak to you from a voice that's not their own? But they remain ever confident, as though they hold some mysterious knowing or secret?"

"You can't let everybody into your thoughts. It's here you need to keep good company."

"If all of what you've been exposed to in a 24-hour day is filth, vile language, hateful behaviors, broken relationships, and bad parenting, how could you expect anything of high value to grow from such a low vibration?"

"The shit I tell you is not because you don't know. It's quite the opposite. It's because you already know. I'm just igniting it in you by shining a light on it."

"You can't live in my shadow if you're standing on top of my shoulders."

"Broken we may be but what keeps us from falling apart?"

"What is a word that leaves a closed door unlocked and gives others entry?"

"People who search for happiness outside of themselves are searching for disappointment."

"How many days as a child did you spend chasing your shadow before realizing that your shadow is you?"

"We spend a lifetime focused on what we don't have and never appreciating what we do have."

"Lighten up and lose the rocks. They were meant for you to gain strength by lifting them out of your way. They were not meant for you to carry."

"Don't be so tribal that you miss out on the opportunity to build a nation."

"The truest gift ever given is one that enables you to extend your roots fully and embrace those you love completely."

"If life is your teacher, be open to finding an opportunity inside of an upset. Not every upset ends in a defeat and not every victory begins with a win."

"True victory is never in the win. It's in how you handle the defeat. A real victory can't come until you've suffered a loss. Only after experiencing a loss will you able to appreciate a win, knowing the difference."

"I think some would believe that my stillness speaks to a greater resilience present in me. Not true. I sit in silence listening to the beauty of God's presence magnified through you."

"You have to go through it to grow through it."

"The only touch any of us ever remember came from a heavy hand. It's hard to remember the hugs after an ass whipping."

"Fear is the virus ravaging and upsetting the world. Lowering your vibration gives it access."

"The old ways exist in being. Anything else is simply theatre."

"No one can be anyone's sole source of energy and support."

"We go through life driving with our foot on the brakes. Uncertain of what's ahead and not having the sensation of a clear direction, we spin our wheels attached to our uncertainty and going nowhere fast."

"People are good at wanting you to exercise patience when you have a need but let them have a need. Watch them make the world stop just so they can quench their thirst."

"If the heaven you've created for yourself has locks and doors, please know you're still in hell. You are just hiding, thinking you're in a safe space."

"If we are to survive the hell we are in, we must create our own frameworks, systems, structures, and containers. We must build our own arks for the storm we are in and for the storms to come to protect us and keep us safe."

"Don't breathe life into something you don't want to exist. Oftentimes, we are the ones that give air to what has passed and been laid to rest. Not everything deserves another opportunity at living."

"Our work for pay is consensual servitude. These chains are unseen and harder to break."

"When you decide to walk alone, walk in your light. If not, you walk in your shadows, having left your mirrors buried behind."

"Hold on to your flowers as hard as you embrace your weeds. Unless your weeds are your flowers!"

"Don't attach yourself to an upset. Especially when someone purposely extends an invitation. Politely refuse and let them smolder inside of their own stew."

"When someone or something says to you in a dream, "You must go back to the old ways," they mean you must be, in spirit, the embodiment of what it is you wish to learn. Doing anything else is simply theatre."

STAY LIT BY DARNELL P. SMITH

4 CONNECTION TO NATURE

"There are walking dead living amongst us. People so in tune with the music of the crown that they're easily led astray. Enchanted by the music of the Pied Piper and the collective vibration of the crowd, they're hypnotized and disconnected from the rhythms of their own hearts. Unconsciously, they work and live like ants and in service to an understanding that's not their own. Their mental and physical sensibilities have been corrupted by a virus that has snatched their bodies away. It's strange seeing humans act this way. Even worse, seeing the world change into a living cemetery."

"How do we alter the landscape of where we live? By leveling the ground and removing the rocks, garbage, and weeds. By tilling, turning, and watering the soil. Likewise, we must alter the landscape of our body, heart, and mind. We must remove the thoughts that lay like hot rocks, remove the stresses that continuously take shape, and whose roots strangle our veins. We must exercise our bodies, learning to breathe properly. We must keep ourselves hydrated and consume foods rich in vital nutrients. We are our own master. Let us now live as such, so we can blossom and bear the fruit of our Creator's calling and of our co-design!"

"None of us are expendable, yet all of us are expendable. What purpose did our Creator input into our design? What are we supposed to bring into fruition and have blossom from our being into this world? We were designed for a specific purpose. It is our calling. It is our value. It is what we live for and it's also what we are called upon if needed to die for. At the end of our service, let the Creator's presence be magnified a thousand times and in response, let the Ancestors greet us with applause shouting, "Job well done!"

"Our collective vibration is rising. Embrace that wave and that feel-good feeling. Rise above your fears. Make this new sensation your new familiar. Make this your new low so that when you stand, your crown rises above the clouds and what you embrace is the warmth of the Sun!"

"I don't know about you, but I've had some low moments in my life. Moments where I was told not to stand, moments where I didn't have the strength to stand, and moments where I was hit hard and laid out by life and couldn't stand. Yet, through all of my lows, despite feeling the cold of night, I've also been embraced by the Sun, raised, and bathed by its light, and comforted by its warmth."

"In a Universe that is infinite in all directions, which way is truly up, and which way is truly down? Our own sense of placement exists in relationship to our planet and sun. The only certainty of any direction is in realizing we are each at its center."

"The light that illuminates our future is sourced from an ancient energy, spiraling forward from our past. Like a train of sorts, it follows a particular pattern. A direction with many stops representing different stages. Every stage is a portal. So, let us embrace being present in the moment and consider our task with being lit, so that we can travel the rails of light illuminated by our Ancestors."

"Dig deep and embrace the beauty of the star that you are. Illuminating your darkness and revealing your power. Your skin is the tapestry of the Universe, and the scroll upon which its secrets are written. Your existence is God's gift, for which I bow and give thanks!"

"Mankind soon faces an eviction. Mama Earth, like any good parent, extends love and grace, but when you become boisterous, loud, and ignorant, termination of lease is imminent."

"None of us are promised tomorrow, so let us fully embrace today. Let our every moment be an opportunity to get clean and clear, so we might be present. Let us embrace the storms, come what may, for what is sure to follow is the Sun casting its light upon us, revealing the most beautiful day."

"To the ancestors and angelic beings, we are no more than what we are… human. As they peer through the interdimensional glass walls, observing us in our every move. Yes, every move! You think they care if you have sex, shit, belch, or pass gas? In your human form, you are no more than the horse, cat, or dog that they love."

"As you ascend, you tighten the netting inside your container, calling forth all sorts of assistance from angels and elevated beings. You bring blessings, not only upon yourself, but to both family and friends. You are the seed from which a thought takes form, elevating humanity simply by being. Salvation is an energetic reaction, brought forth by those caught in the wave of your wind. Your awakened presence is the revelation of the coming of Christ in you, through you, as you. For this, we give thanks!"

"Why do religious leaders eclipse the Sun and bathe in its rays while leaving you shaking in their shadows when you to have a direct connect with his Son?"

"Knowledge is infinite but our capacity to understand is not. We are limited by the container that we are in. The depth and width of our understanding is likened to the memory contained on a computer drive. Our storage capacity like a computer, although vast, is limited. Not until we give up our bodies does the opportunity to embrace what is infinite become possible."

"You are a cell in the body of the universe. Your creation was with purpose. You are not a mistake. You are indispensable to the forward movement of the world."

"Too often, we pour into people that don't pour back into us. We are the faucet, and they are the drain. It is a give and take relationship. This notion that we are to give freely without thought, expectation, or demand from the beneficiary is a notion created by an enslaver. When we give to people that don't give back to us, we permit our life force to be drained by vampires that are there for the taking and there for the feeding. They are like lotuses that are there to steal the harvest.

In a well-balanced healthy environment, everything has a compliment. Giving to those that give creates a vortex that indirectly feeds all participants. The exchange of energy moves so rapidly and increases so strongly that wealth is its by-product. When all the elements of nature come together, in a critical mass, we have harvested. The law of reciprocity is a golden rule to live by. Do unto others as you would want others to do unto you. Honor those that honor you. Feed those that feed you. Give to those that give to you. Love those that love you. This energy exchange has a name: synergy and true family."

"We are generations of men and women bred to turn a blind eye on the injustices suffered by one another. From Cape Coast to Plymouth Rock, from sunup to sundown, we've had to endure atrocities no other human being would subject another. Worse than witnessing the suffering and torment of others is having to turn a blind eye. In doing so, we have abandoned and lost our greatest strength, which is empathy. We have severed the cords of our connection and we have unknowingly chosen individualism, which for our people is synonymous with death."

"Uncertainty has us. No clear direction to travel. No assurance of heaven and, if what has us ain't hell, we choose the misery of this life without wanting any sudden reservation to a place possibly worse. This confusion has us in every way. Even when we pray, we find God's silence deafening. Yet, we innately understand there's an uncertain victory. We just have to push through in the right direction and then possibly we can decode life's mystery."

"We stand before the world lost and blind to the blessings before us, unable to see past our own shadows. The light within us only gravitates toward its own reflection. The images that our light mirrors in the world. If a blessing is what you truly desire, give attention to the thread of light within you. It will navigate you through your darkness and will connect you with an image of brightness. It's a reflection within the world."

"You can pour into everyone else's cup, but it doesn't mean that anyone will pour into yours. But rest assured, if you are on your path, the universe will provide. The law of reciprocity is always in full effect."

"Let us discover what it truly means to be connected. To be one family, one village, or one nation. We are like droplets of water that merged together, becoming one puddle, one lake, one river, one ocean, and one container. Yes, we simply consist of droplets of water, whole and complete, representing one body with a multitude of personalities housed under one conscious."

"So many of us occupy these spaces where we feel no gratitude at all. No gratitude for the food we eat, for the clothing we wear, for the shelter we have, for the air we breathe, for the coolness of the night, or for the warmth of the sun. We claim never to have asked for it, as though we played no part in the selection of our circumstance, no part in our own creation, and no ownership of our own becoming. I'd like to say that we each need to wake the "F" up and take ownership of our own becoming and have gratitude for where we stand. Our Creator graced us with life. All we need to do is Be!"

"Be blessed!" This saying is the great equalizer. A prayer for both enemy and friend to rise to their highest self. A summoning for them to go through whatever heaven or hell is required to reach their divinity. It is a release of responsibility for the speaker. A request for divine intervention on behalf of those who know not what's needed to make up the difference. When confronted with a situation or person, for whom you have no answer to address their confusion, simply saying "*be blessed*" is calling upon a higher power. Setting your mind and spirit free from the weight of what ills them."

"The greatest challenge before us is not in winning. It is in being. In not cowering before the world, but in being a beacon of light, summoning the Sun in each and every one!"

"The remnants of a weed lodged in the soil of our mind only requires a smidgeon of light to spark new growth. Be a mindful gardener tending to the threshold of your thought, directing your Sun to radiate rays of light on health, wellness, opportunity, and bliss."

"If you descend into darkness, you might discover the Creator's likeness in you. Shine bright!"

"The choices that some of us make are unfortunate. Swearing up and down how much we love the Lord, but when the power of Creation stands before us, who do we choose? We never choose what's ultimate. Instead, we embrace the lower Lords of pain, grief, anger, and fear but never choosing in what we claim is most dear. Smh."

"There are occasions when we have to choose what is unclean to sustain us. For instance, if you've ever been thirsty like you've been in the desert for five days, it wouldn't matter where your water came from. As long as it quenches your thirst and hydrates your depleted body. So, what happens when you thirst for light and when you thirst for Spirit? When what's inside you craves for the presence of our Creator? When what's inside you seeks the warmth of the Sun? You would do like most. You'd grab whatever morsel, whatever crumb, whatever thread of light this presence hung from, to silence your crave and to fill it's warmth."

"Your light was never meant to be consumed by darkness. It was meant to dance with darkness, for you are a star in the night."

"You are more than sufficient! You are divine dust. The Creator's breath spoke you into existence."

"It used to be that we poured into those things that gave back to us. Nowadays, we direct our attention to everything except what feeds us."

"Holding space for another isn't necessarily descending into the hell that they're in. It's quite the opposite. It's positioning yourself in such a way that you anchor yourself so that you can pull them out, if needed, without falling in."

"When we collapse domains, we indirectly allow the stench of others to muddy our own waters. With this being the case, be mindful of what energy you open your doors to. Be mindful, for without barriers, we allow the stench of others to pollute our waters."

"God is always talking. We just were never trained on how to listen. We're so wrapped up with what's going on outside ourselves, we can never tune in and make sense of the ambient silence and sounds that dwell within."

"What pains one is what impacts us all. The nerves that make up our inner body are also connected to the vibratory field of our planet's outer body. We're all plugged in, so what affects one indirectly, affects us all."

"If there is no enemy within, the enemy without can do you no harm."

"Who do you trust when all who stood before you betrayed you? When all you would call "friend" never extended a hand to raise you? When those who you call "mom", "dad", and "family", tasked with showing you the right way, were fed poison and lies that they then feed you. Who do you trust when it seems not even the Creator responded to your cries? Even so, we must pause and give thanks. Because it's in this all-consuming storm that has become our life that our Creator uses these elements of this world to bring forth his light. Inside of you lies an answer and through you, there will come a solution. You are God sent and simply cast in the fires of this life, not to be beaten, burned, or defeated, but to have your flame molded in such a way that it repels the wickedness of this world away. These fires give rise to your presence deep inside. It's here that you discover your light."

"All things work together toward a greater good. Unbeknownst to Satan, even he is a servant of our Creator."

"If it takes a crew of sailors to operate a vessel, how many spirits does it require to operate you? What consciousness directs your organs, cells, and other automated functions of your body, beyond your conscious control? What other entities are at work in the avatar that is you?"

"What motivates you to serve your Creator? A sense of love, purpose, and forgiveness? Or is it power, fear, or obedience? Whatever your rationale or reason, your belief is only as strong as your connection."

"Navigate your vessel. Give it direction. Have an intent. It will power you through the storms of life that will come."

"Command both your action and reaction to circumstances. Your power is in your response. Or fall victim to the wind, waves, and rain when they come… crashing your vessel against the rocks."

"Being still for many is death. But all of us are required to unplug and check-in with something greater from time to time."

"What is death but a portal from one existence to another?"

"External forces are always at work, attempting to divert us from fulfilling our mission, purpose, and passion. Whatever the agent of distraction, welcome it as a friend that is meant to strengthen you, not to break you."

"True happiness and bliss exist. But sometimes, you have to dance through the challenges of life to peel back the layers of protection that you have purposely placed before it. Only then can you rise and embrace your brightness from within."

"As a child, I feared death and hated God for what I thought was a cruel joke: being born to die. Death was an inevitable conclusion to existing and all roads accelerated or delayed this becoming. As an adult, I've learned to love life and what I fear is God's absence. Death is no longer an enemy, but the inevitable conclusion of a life well lived and a rebirth into something greater."

"Life is a team sport that requires each person to play their position. When we fail to communicate any shortcoming or misgiving, we set ourselves and our team up for failure. The only thing worse than not showing up is having those who are reliant on your presence to ponder the reasons for your absence, as they commence to engage the battles before them, crippled by your absence."

"Making a difference in someone's life isn't always about maintaining a connection. Often, it's knowing when and how to let go with love."

"Through your words, I and others rise. Words are empty unless possessed by a spirit in your breath. You have the power to heal, hurt, lift and simply from the intent of your speech. Understand the power you are and act accordingly. Be intentional with this air we share."

"We are each engineers, architects, and builders crafting our designs. Divinely, intelligently, or recklessly. Our very nature commands that we create. The challenge is in our ability to tap into our divine intelligence, especially when we've been trained to believe that the source of knowledge comes from outside of us rather than through us. Consider this fact: if every other animal on the planet has an instinct and a knowing, why would our Creator not have given the same to us?"

"Let us stand as spirits inhabiting bodies, fulfilling our calling in covenant with our Creator's life force that shines through us, as us."

"We were born to experience love, laughter, community, and care. This social anxiety that exists around lack is a sensation not born of our DNA. Even in the midst of having nothing, our presence influences everything. We are the difference and the sum. Our presence powers this Universe. We are kin to the sun."

"Everything in nature is programmed by the Most High. Know that what our Creator has put into the Earth is greater than what man can duplicate in labs. Man understands life's mechanics, but he is clueless to the energy that powers it."

"If you fear God, check yourself. Only predators and those who mean you harm should awaken fear. The only fear one should have of God is God's absence. If you're in a perpetual state of fear, check your connection. In times of difficulty, when you have nothing to turn to, God's presence may awaken in you. It is here, despite your difficulty, in your discovery, that you find comfort. God is love and God's love is real."

"God's riches flow through us. Through us, we illuminate God's presence. Our bodies are God's pipeline to the world."

"Until the heart chakra is awakened and assumes power, there can be no inner peace."

"We cannot begin to see until we are able to walk through our pain, decoding the messages that lie within, and understanding our Creator's intent in the shaping of our lives. This has us realizing the reasoning for our deep dive into the hell we are in, awakening to our shared purpose of being animated vessels of our Creator's presence. Knowing that we are spirit-filled vessels, meant to brave the fires of Earth. Resurrecting heaven in this hell we are in by being and embracing our own illumination."

"Information is not discovered. It is revealed. As humans, we can tap into the intelligence of the Universe. What we see, hear, touch, and smell are our body sensors decoding what we already know. Yes, all that you recognize, good and bad, are sensations that inform a knowingness buried deep within us, awaiting the moment we decipher their coding. Giving birth to wisdom contained in the ether of our soul."

"If you're in a dark space and conscious of it, you're awake to the reality that you're alone, disconnected, and lost. In this instance, fear has you and finding safety is your pursuit. It's here in this moment at the crossroads of your existence that the consequences of your every decision finds you. Know your every action will be judged a blessing or a curse, as our Creator helps to navigate you home. Being with our Creator, awakened in your body is your triumph. The realization that you are never alone is both your bounty and gift."

STAY LIT BY DARNELL P. SMITH

Author Index

Using your smartphone, open your camera and scan this code to access Darnell P. Smith's information hub to stay connected and up to date with future books, projects, and endeavors.

www.ingramcontent.com/pod-product-compliance
Lightning Source LLC
Chambersburg PA
CBHW060450030426
42337CB00015B/1530